This Jacana book belongs to:

____

This book was made possible with support and funding from the National Arts Council.

First published by Jacana Media (Pty) Ltd in 2023

10 Orange Street
Sunnyside
Auckland Park 2092
South Africa
+2711 628 3200

ISBN 978-1-4314-3377-3

Set in LiebeRuth 17/21pt
Printed by ABC Press, Cape Town
Job no. 004069

For a complete list of Jacana titles visit www.jacana.co.za

The Joy Dancer

Gregory Maqoma & Gcina Mhlophe

Illustrated by Elizabeth Pulles

JACANA
CHILDREN'S
BOOKS

Gregory loved going into the dusty streets of Soweto
to play with his friends.

"Mama, I'm going to play outside."

"Be back by dinner time, Gregory."

"Please keep the empty shoe polish tin for me, Mama?
I need two more wheels for my new wire car."

He waved goodbye and ran out to join his friends.

"We own the streets! This street is for
our feet!" they shouted loudly.

On weekends their house was usually filled
with music.

"I love your jazz music, Tata," said Gregory.

"Good. Why don't you choose a record,"
said his father.

Gregory chose an album.

When the music played, he swayed from side
to side. He did not dare to dance. His father
would get angry if he did.

This music makes me feel like I am a bird,
ready to fly on spirit wings. One day, he
thought, one day I will be a famous dancer.

On Sunday, Gregory wanted to go down to the men's
hostel. He saw Vincent in the street.

"I want to watch the BaPedi dancers and the BaSotho
men singing," he said. "Come with me. We'll push our
way through the crowd to get to the front."

When the whistle sounded the dancers moved forward.
Both boys watched and tried to remember every move
that the dancers made.

"When we're back home," Vincent shouted,
"we'll try some of their moves."

"Yes, and maybe use some of my Tata's jazz."

"Gregory, you spend far too much time reading."

"It is important that you get some exercise too," said his mother.

"I've tried soccer, but I don't enjoy it."

"Reading is important for your studies,"
said his father.

"I'm sorry you didn't like soccer, but
now I want you to join the marching
band."

"The what?"

"The marching band. You will be
playing the big drum."

Gregory dared not say a word.

Soon Gregory was playing the big drum and enjoying himself. One day he spoke to the drum majorettes.

"I can teach you some new steps if you like."

"Yes, please. We all know you can dance," the girls squealed with excitement.

"Eish, Greg," said Vincent, "people just love your style."

"I don't know where these ideas come from, Vince. They just jump into my mind."

Very soon they were winning many competitions. More and more people invited them to perform.

One day a friend in the marching band called him over.

"I have a brilliant idea," said Mpho. "Why don't we form
a small group? Just the three of us."

"Why not?" said Gregory. "We can call it 'The Joy Dancers'."

"I like that! You can count me in," said Vincent.

From the day they started they became well known
in the township.

"Wow, we've even been asked to dance at a wedding,"
said Gregory. "And a school concert."

"Someone suggested that we call ourselves 'Michael
Jackson's African Family'," said Vincent.

"No thanks," said Gregory with a smile. "I like The Joy
Dancers. It's like my name Vuyani, which means be
happy, and dancing makes us happy."

"Gregory."

"Yes, Tata."

"Why don't you want to go to school?"

"I'm scared. There are soldiers in the school,
watching us."

"I understand. Look at the newspaper. You will
see that people are protesting."

Gregory slowly paged through the newspaper.
Suddenly he grabbed one page and ran
out of the door.

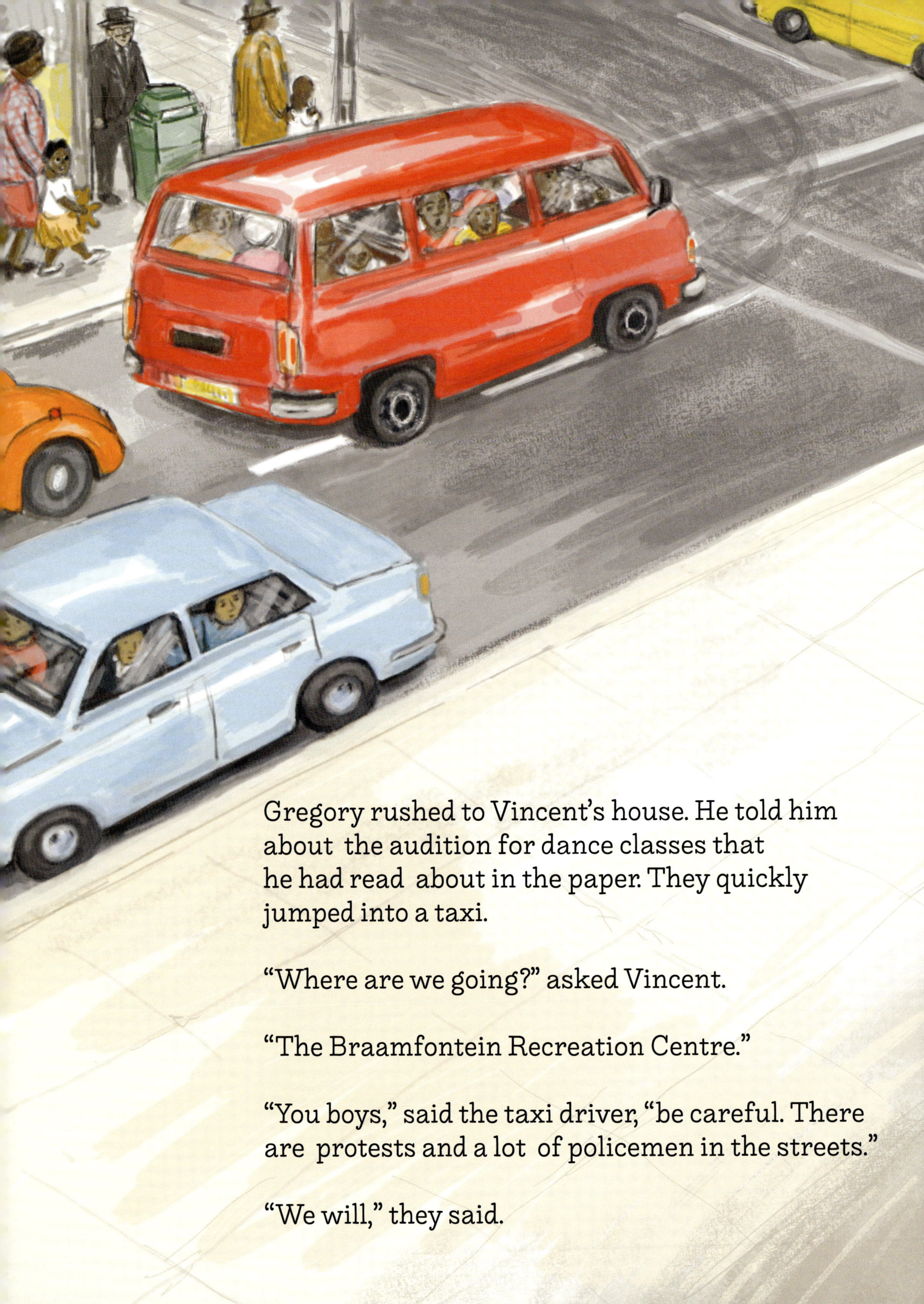

Gregory rushed to Vincent's house. He told him
about the audition for dance classes that
he had read about in the paper. They quickly
jumped into a taxi.

"Where are we going?" asked Vincent.

"The Braamfontein Recreation Centre."

"You boys," said the taxi driver, "be careful. There
are protests and a lot of policemen in the streets."

"We will," they said.

POLISIE
END

When they looked into the hall
their mouths fell open.
"Let's go. This is not for us,"
Vincent said.

But they stayed.

They were accepted at the
Moving into Dance classes.

"YOH! What great news,
Vince," said Gregory.

"And a one-year scholarship,"
said Vincent.

"I can't believe it. It's Sylvia
Glasser's school — everyone
wants to study with her!"

Every afternoon, month after month,
they went to dance classes.

Gregory was always worried that
his father would find out and stop
him from going.

It worked out well for a time until
the newspaper article.

When he walked into the lounge, he saw his father reading the newspaper. There, in the middle of the page, was a photograph of him and Vincent ... dancing.

Now what? He waited for the explosion.

"Will you look at this," his father asked the
neighbour. "Have you seen the newspaper?
My son is in it," he said proudly.

"Well, well, well. So many people really like this
jiving of yours, Gregory. But just remember you
still have to study mathematics or science at
university. That is more important."

Gregory simply nodded and did not say anything.

Eventually Gregory's time at school was over.

It took all his courage to go to his father. "Tata, I applied to university, but there is no scholarship." He waited for the explosion. There was none.

"I have been offered a full scholarship for a one-year dance course."

Gregory could not believe his ears when his parents agreed. He was so happy. His heart was dancing faster than his feet ever could.

There was so much he learnt in the months he was there.

Then the bad luck arrived. He injured his knee. Gregory had to stop dancing.

Not only that, he also had to find a job.

For two long years he wore a suit and worked in an office.

And then, at last, a ray of hope shone through. Vincent contacted him.

"I've been invited to go on a six-week dance tour all over Africa. And you're coming with me."

"WHAT? I'm leaving my job right now!"

He packed his suitcase and was off.

From then on Gregory felt that his light was shining brighter every day.

Gregory and Vincent travelled and danced
from country to country in Africa.

"Vince," Gregory said when the tour ended,
"I applied for a scholarship at a special dance
school in Belgium. I got in."

Vincent laughed. "Of course, you did."

Gregory is still dancing today. He has received many awards.

He opened the Vuyani Dance Theatre in 1999 and is known
all over the world for his dancing and his shows.

He hopes that the people who watch him dance feel the story he
is trying to tell. He loves to connect to the rhythm of his ancestors.